D1305744

Fractions in Color

by Margaret Fetty

STECK-VAUGHN

Harcourt Supplemental Publishers

www.steck-vaughn.com

Have you ever shared a snack with a friend?
To share fairly, you break things into **equal parts**.
Fractions name parts of a whole.

Fractions can help us be fair when we share!
Colors can help make fractions easier to see.

Here is a group of raincoats.
There are two raincoats in all.
What fraction of the raincoats are **blue?**
What fraction of the raincoats are **red?**

How to Think About Fractions

The group of raincoats has **two** equal parts.
The group shows **halves**.

One raincoat is blue.
So **one half** of the group is blue.

$$\frac{1}{2}$$

One raincoat is red.
So **one half** of the group is red.

$$\frac{1}{2}$$

Here is a group of floats.
There are three floats in all.
What fraction of the floats are **purple?**
What fraction of the floats are **green?**

How to Think About Fractions

The group of floats has **three** equal parts.
The group shows **thirds**.

One float is purple.
So **one third** of the group is purple.

$$\frac{1}{3}$$

Two floats are green.
So **two thirds** of the group are green.

$$\frac{2}{3}$$

Here is a group of juice pops.
There are four juice pops in all.
What fraction of the juice pops are **green**?
What fraction of the juice pops are **pink**?

How to Think About Fractions

The group of juice pops has **four** equal parts.
The group shows **fourths**.

One juice pop is green.
So **one fourth** of the group is green.

$$\frac{1}{4}$$

Three juice pops are pink.
So **three fourths** of the group are pink.

$$\frac{3}{4}$$

Here is a group of apples.
There are five apples in all.
What fraction of the apples are **red**?
What fraction of the apples are **green**?

How to Think About Fractions

The group of apples has **five** equal parts.
The group shows **fifths**.

One apple is red.
So **one fifth** of the group is red.

$$\frac{1}{5}$$

Four apples are green.
So **four fifths** of the group are green.

$$\frac{4}{5}$$

Here is a group of birds.
There are five birds in all.
What fraction of the birds are **green**?
What fraction of the birds are **blue**?

How to Think About Fractions

The group of birds has **five** equal parts.
The group shows **fifths** again.

Two birds are green.
So **two fifths** of the group are green.

$$\frac{2}{5}$$

Three birds are blue.
So **three fifths** of the group are blue.

$$\frac{3}{5}$$

Here is a group of flowers.
There are six flowers in all.
What fraction of the flowers are **pink**?
What fraction of the flowers are **purple**?

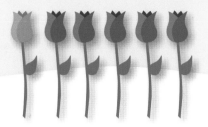

How to Think About Fractions

The group of flowers has **six** equal parts.
The group shows **sixths**.

One flower is pink.
So **one sixth** of the group is pink.

$$\frac{1}{6}$$

Five flowers are purple.
So **five sixths** of the group are purple.

$$\frac{5}{6}$$

Here is a group of fish.
There are six fish in all.
What fraction of the fish are **blue?**
What fraction of the fish are orange?

How to Think About Fractions

The group of fish has **six** equal parts.
The group shows **sixths** again.

Two fish are blue.
So **two sixths** of the group are blue.

$$\frac{2}{6}$$

Four fish are orange.
So **four sixths** of the group are orange.

$$\frac{4}{6}$$

Here is a group of balloons.
There are six balloons in all.
What fraction of the balloons are **green**?
What fraction of the balloons are **purple**?

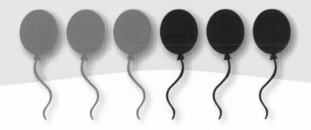

How to Think About Fractions

The group of balloons has **six** equal parts.
Here is another way to show **sixths**.

Three balloons are green.
So **three sixths** of the group are green.

$$\frac{3}{6}$$

Three balloons are purple.
So **three sixths** of the group are purple.

$$\frac{3}{6}$$

Here is a group of cupcakes.
There are seven cupcakes in all.
What fraction of the cupcakes have **brown** icing?
What fraction of the cupcakes have **pink** icing?

How to Think About Fractions

The group of cupcakes has **seven** equal parts.
The group shows **sevenths**. ✶

Three cupcakes have brown icing.
So **three sevenths** of the group have brown icing.

$$\frac{3}{7}$$

Four cupcakes have pink icing.
So **four sevenths** of the group have pink icing.

$$\frac{4}{7}$$

Here is a group of seven candles.
What fraction of the candles are **red?**
What fraction of the candles are **black?**
What fraction of the candles are **green?**

How to Think About Fractions

The group of candles has **seven** equal parts.
The group shows **sevenths** again.

Three candles are red.
So **three sevenths** of the group are red.

$$\frac{3}{7}$$

One candle is black.
So **one seventh** of the group is black.

$$\frac{1}{7}$$

Three candles are green.
So **three sevenths** of the group are green.

$$\frac{3}{7}$$

Take a look around.
The world is filled with fractions.
What other **fractions in color** can you find?